Genealogy in Reverse: Finding the Living

A Practical Guide for All Genealogists

I0160809

By
Cheri Hudson Passey

Genealogical Publishing Company

ISBN 9780806321516

Published by Genealogical Publishing Company
Baltimore, Maryland
2025

Dedication

This book is dedicated to our soldiers who are still missing and the families who yearn to bring them home.

And to the Roberts brothers, Wilbert, Gilbert, and Edman, killed within a few months of each other during WWII.
Thank you for your service.
Heroes each.

Left to Right: Edman, Wilbert and Gilbert Roberts
(Original Photo in Possession of Author)

Edman Roberts
(Original Photo in Possession of Author)

Edman, may my work be paying it forward to the day we bring you home.

Contents

About the Author

Cheri Hudson Passey is a professional genealogist, instructor, writer, speaker, and owner of Carolina Girl Genealogy, LLC. She hosts the "GenFriends Genealogy Chat Show on YouTube where she and a panel of professional genealogists meet weekly to discuss all things genealogy.

Cheri began working as a genealogical researcher subcontracted by Eagle Investigative Services, Inc., for the US Army Past Conflict Repatriations Branch in December of 2018. She uses her skills to identify and locate the next of kin, along with YDNA and mtDNA candidates from the family of WWII soldiers who are listed as missing in action. The goal is to use DNA to positively identify remains and, with the permission of next of kin, bring our war heroes home.

Cheri contacts family members who in many instances have heard the soldier's story and are anxious to help with identification and bring their family member home where they belong. Daughters, sons, brothers and sisters for some soldiers have lived long lives and are thrilled to hear a case has been opened for their loved ones.

More often nephews, nieces and family farther down the line are those who are alive and can help with a case. Many are the keepers of the family memorabilia and have awards, medals and other personal items of the soldier. Talking to them and explaining the project as well as listening to their stories make this work fulfilling.

In 2024, Cheri was contacted by a researcher from another repatriation company who was working on a case opened for her great uncle. Edman Roberts, her maternal grandfather's brother, was listed as missing in action in 1944. His plane went down in Sicily and his remains were not found. She was able to give information on how the genealogist could contact the primary and secondary next of kin for Edman and those who would be DNA connections.

This case is ongoing, and she hopes his remains will be brought home to be buried in the empty grave next to his two brothers, one of them her grandfather, who also died during the war.

Preface

Genealogy often feels like a treasure hunt, piecing together the stories of those who came before us. But sometimes the focus shifts from the past to the present as we look for living relatives who can fill in the gaps in our family stories. Perhaps you are building your family tree, helping others trace their roots, looking for DNA connections for reasons like discovering an adoptee's biological parent, or finding cousins to help move your tree back generations, or working on special projects like military repatriations, or finding descendants of an enslaved community. Learning how to find living relatives can be a valuable skill to help you reach out and connect with living family and descendants of your ancestors who may have the information you are looking for or be able to put you in touch with those who do.

This book aims to help genealogists at every level learn to trace descendants of ancestors, both direct line and collateral. With step-by-step guidance, methodologies, and practical examples, this guide will give you the tools and confidence to find and make meaningful connections with living family members.

Methodology

Finding living relatives isn't all that different from tracing your direct-line ancestors and their families. The same skills apply—researching, organizing information, and following clues—but with a focus on connecting the past to the present. This process, known as reverse genealogy, involves creating a detailed family tree, identifying relatives down both ancestral and collateral lines, and using modern tools to track them down.

Steps for finding a living family member include:

1. Ensuring the line you are researching is as correct as possible.

2. Researching generations up the tree and then back down on collateral lines.

3. Analyzing and correlating information to correctly identify a living descendant and locate contact information.

4. Using best practices for contacting and sharing information.

The following chapters will discuss these steps and give examples of working through them. In time, you will develop the skills necessary and find a pattern of locating the living that works for you.

Chapter 1:
Building a Solid Foundation

The first step in finding living relatives is ensuring your family tree is accurate and complete. Start by documenting your direct ancestors, their children, siblings, and all known spouses. Add biological family and step- or adopted people, too. Collateral relatives are anyone who is connected to your ancestors and their family and often are the ones who lead to modern-day family members. These are brothers, sisters, aunts, uncles, cousins, step and adopted people in your family tree.

You want to spread your tree far and wide to look for those who can help you on your quest to find those who can help you. Remember to gather information about who is recorded in records as having lived with or appears to have a close tie to family members. Boarders, housekeepers, laborers, and others may be family or very close friends and can lead you to unknown records and new connections.

Consider creating a separate tree or twig for the line you want descendants of. It will help you stay focused and organized.

You can create smaller trees for reverse searching on genealogy websites like Ancestry.com, FamilySearch.com, MyHeritage.com, or Findmypast.com. You can do it manually by starting a new tree and then adding the family you are researching a person at a time, or using genealogy computer software to split the line and upload the new GEDCOM file to the website you work with.

To use computer software programs like Family Tree Maker, Legacy Family Tree, or RootsMagic to split your line, you will need to import a GEDCOM file- the file type for family trees. For instance, if you use Ancestry, go to your tree and click on "tree info." from there, click on the "Export Tree" link. You will then have a GEDCOM file for your tree downloaded to your computer.

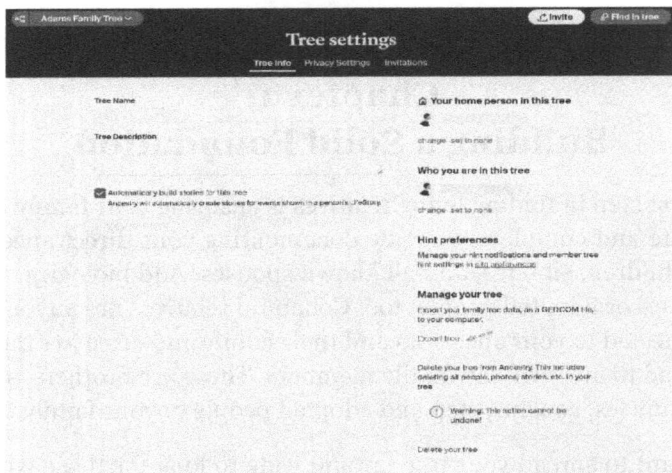

Screenshot of Export Link from Ancestry

You can then upload the file into your software program by clicking the "Import" tab and selecting the file you want to upload.

Screenshot of Legacy Family Tree Import/Export Buttons

If you already use one of these programs, you most likely have a GED-COM file downloaded into it. If you don't have a genealogy software program on your computer, you can look for an option to try the program for free. Look for free versions on their websites, download and then create a GEDCOM file from the website your tree is on, and then import it to your program using the "Import" option under Files.

To create a smaller tree, go to the "Export" option in your software, choose the name of the person whose line you want to split off. Then, select from the options of who else to include. You will want the person at the top of the line that you want to focus on and their descendants. Each software program has these choices, but their wording may be different.

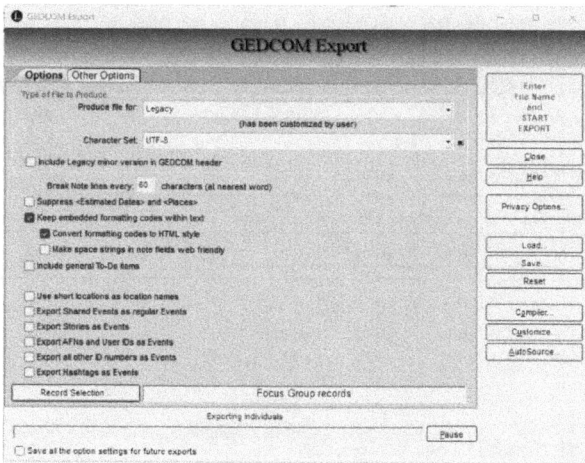

Screenshot of Legacy Family Tree Software Record
Selection Options

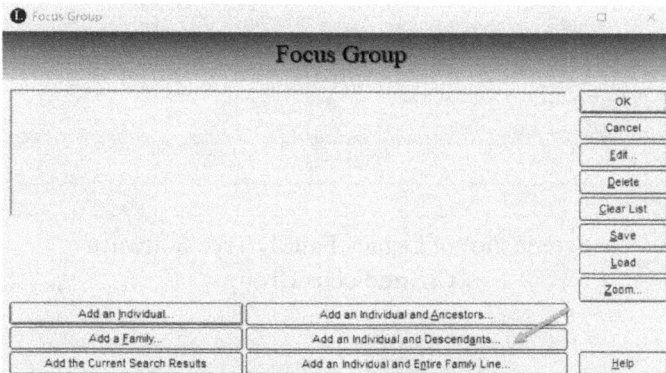

Screenshot of Legacy Family Tree Software

Focus Group Record Choices

13

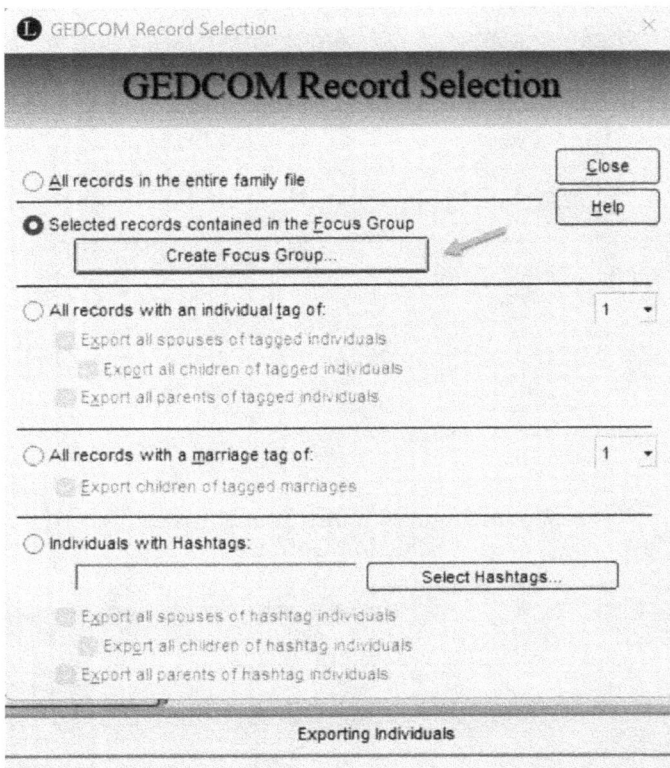

GEDCOM Record Selection

GEDCOM Record Selection

○ All records in the entire family file

● Selected records contained in the Focus Group

　　Create Focus Group...

○ All records with an individual tag of:　　1 ▾

　　☐ Export all spouses of tagged individuals
　　☐ Export all children of tagged individuals
　　☐ Export all parents of tagged individuals

○ All records with a marriage tag of:　　1 ▾

　　☐ Export children of tagged marriages

○ Individuals with Hashtags:

　　[　　　　　　　　　　]　Select Hashtags...

　　☐ Export all spouses of hashtag individuals
　　☐ Export all children of hashtag individuals
　　☐ Export all parents of hashtag individuals

Close

Help

Exporting Individuals

Screenshot of Legacy Family Tree Software
Create Focus Group

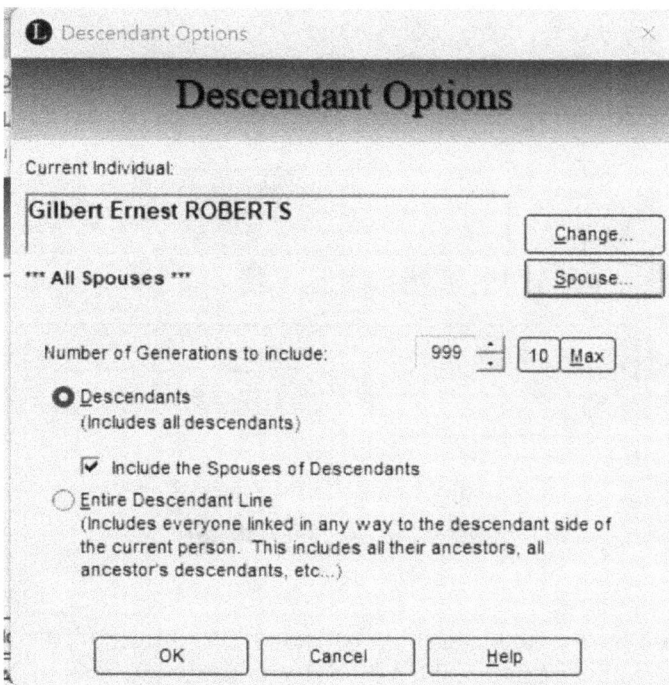

Descendant Options

Current Individual:

Gilbert Ernest ROBERTS

[Change...]

*** All Spouses ***

[Spouse...]

Number of Generations to include: 999 ⇅   [10] [Max]

○ Descendants
(Includes all descendants)

   ☑ Include the Spouses of Descendants

○ Entire Descendant Line
(Includes everyone linked in any way to the descendant side of
the current person. This includes all their ancestors, all
ancestor's descendants, etc...)

[OK]   [Cancel]   [Help]

Screenshot of Chosen Line to Split
Legacy Family Tree Software

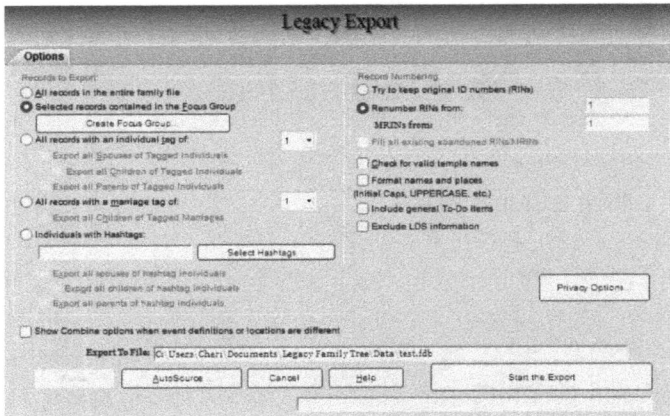

Screenshot of GEDCOM Export Page

Legacy Family Tree Software

Once you have created your new GEDCOM file, return to your genealogy website and then upload the file to create a new tree. Make sure it is labeled to reflect the family of this smaller tree.

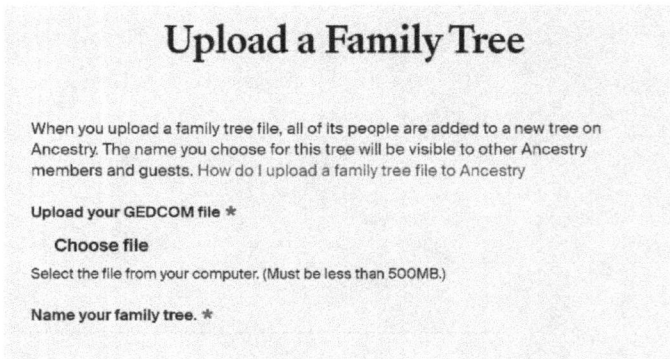

Upload a Family Tree

When you upload a family tree file, all of its people are added to a new tree on Ancestry. The name you choose for this tree will be visible to other Ancestry members and guests. How do I upload a family tree file to Ancestry

Upload your GEDCOM file *

Choose file

Select the file from your computer. (Must be less than 500MB.)

Name your family tree. *

Screenshot of Ancestry Upload Family Tree Page

16

You can also work on your small tree directly from the program. Use links to record collections sites or manually add what you find to your program.

Genealogy websites have extensive historical records collections and tools for building and organizing family trees. A smaller tree will also bring in hints and collaborations specific to the targeted line, making it easier to stay organized, analyze your findings, and correlate information.

One of the advantages of using a genealogy software program to store your tree is having all your information on your computer. Uploading documents, photos, and other information helps keep it safe and not at risk of genealogy websites no longer having these items available. Record providers can cancel their contract with a website, and then they are no longer available online. If you use a one-world tree site such as FamilySearch, all your information is in your program, and no one can change it.

Another plus is the ability to work on your tree from your program and then have your changes sink into your online tree. There are also helps for crafting source citations, research guidance, publishing options, and a place to keep your research notes and plans.

Which genealogy program or website is best? Choose the one that works for you! Just as people differ in whether they use Windows, a Mac, an Android, or an iPhone, try them out using free versions if available and pick the one that thinks like you do.

If you prefer Word, Google Docs, or any other platform to keep the information you collect, that works, too. The important thing is to have a way to save information, citations, and photos and to create a descendant tree for adding people. You will also need a way to analyze what you find in written form.

Include a research plan to stay focused on your goals and keep a log of where you have researched, the location, and what you did or did not discover. Plans and logs can be created within genealogy programs on your computer or any other platform you have chosen to work with. They can be as simple as a Word or Google Document; if you prefer paper, that's ok too.

Writing about your research as you work through the process of finding people is a methodology that can help. On any platform you choose, create a document that you can use to record findings, a clip of the record with its citation, your analysis, and correlation thoughts all in one place. Even if you have to leave your research for a while, you can return to your document and know where you left off.

The steps for this methodology are:

For each record you find:

1. Record the type of record.

2. Add a clip of the part of the record that shows the information about the ancestor.

3. Place a citation underneath the record.

4. Analyze your findings by writing your thoughts about the record, its condition, reliability, and the quality of the information it provides.

5. Look for conflicting information between the information in this record and the ones you have gathered previously. If there is a conflict, write it down and explain how you plan on resolving it.

Do this for each piece of evidence, all on one document, one descendant line at a time. It is a great way to stay organized and focused on the goal of finding living family.

If you are looking for a digital way to keep you on track, Goldie Mae (GoldieMae.com) is a free extension for your computer with an option to pay for more features. When turned on, it automatically records the websites you have researched, creating a log of where you have been. It also includes many other features to help you stay organized, analyze, and correlate your results. It's simple and easy to use.

As you work, follow the **Genealogical Proof Standard (GPS)** to ensure your research is reliable. The GPS was created by the Board for Certification of Genealogists to help all genealogists reach sound conclusions about their genealogy questions.

The elements of the GPS are:

- Performing thorough research in a wide variety of sources. Look for all records that may answer your research question.

- Creating complete and accurate citations for each source. Record who created the record, what the source title is, when the creation date was, where it is in the record page, or volume number is in the record, and where the record is.

- Analyzing and correlating information found in records and documents. Ask yourself about the evidence's quality and condition, why it was created, and whether it seems reliable. It's also important to correlate it with others that you have. Does your information support the previously found data? Is there a conflict.

- Resolving any conflicts found within records. If you find information that conflicts with others, you must resolve the conflict before moving on. Sometimes, it just takes more analysis and correlation and often requires more research.

- Writing conclusions for your research based on strong evidence from incorporating the other elements of the GPS. It helps to understand how you came to your conclusions and shows other researchers your work can be trusted.

These five elements work together to help prevent errors in your research.

A strong, well-researched family tree is your starting point for discovering living relatives; implementing the GPS as you research to find the living will build confidence and help you to discover the correct descendants for the people included in your tree.

Applying the five GPS elements is the key to producing quality work.

Often, I am asked to give an example of a resolved conflict. Here is one:

My great grandfather's headstone gave a date for his death that was in conflict with other records. His death certificate has not been found. I began searching for other records that would have been created at the time of his death and located the funeral home record that recorded his death and burial. Since you don't have a funeral before you die, I was able to resolve the question of his date of death. The headstone was wrong.

Chapter 2:
Looking for Clues in Records

Once you've built your tree, the next step is to look for records that point you to living family members and to help you track them down.

Please note: To protect the privacy of living individuals, all examples of records used in this chapter contain those who are deceased.

Newspapers

Obituaries

Look at obituaries carefully. They often contain many pieces of information that can help you put together the puzzle of a family. You can find out who predeceased and survived the deceased. Where were the living residing at the time of their loved ones's death? Make sure to note the names of spouses. Those will come in handy to help determine if you have the correct person when there are same-named individuals in an area. In older obituaries, women were routinely recorded as Mrs. with their husband's last name. Knowing the name of the spouse and the location will help identify the daughters of the deceased. Record the names of children and grandchildren and any data included about them. Sometimes, only the number of grandchildren, nieces, or nephews is listed. Numbers are still a clue and a hint of descendants of how many there were at their loved one's death. Look for collateral families such as brothers, sisters, aunts, uncles, cousins, etc. Piece the family together as you search for those still living.

Obituaries can help determine biological family when dealing with a blended family and are essential when looking for DNA donors to confirm family relationships. Recently, when looking for which of a deceased man's siblings was eligible to provide mtDNA, I searched for a record to help determine which siblings had the same mother. A conflict in the records linking biological and stepmothers to the children was found in several records. Needing more information to help solve the conflict, I turned to an online obituary for the answer. Only those who were the biological children of the deceased woman were named. Using this information as a clue, I contacted those children and discovered that they were indeed biologically related through their mother and were those needed for mtDNA testing.

Arthur W. Baker Of Sumter Dies

1940

Sumter, Oct. 28.—Arthur Wellington Baker, lifelong resident of Sumter county, died this morning at the Tuomey hospital after a lingering illness.

Born April 28, 1857, he was the son of Mary Jones and Alpheus Baker.

He is survived by his widow, Martha Bradford Baker, and the following children: J. A. Baker, Charlotte; Mrs. J. R. Early and Mrs. J. T. Wells of Columbia, Mrs. J. P. Ryan, Sumter; also two brothers, J. M. Baker and Wilder Baker of Lynchburg; three sisters, Mrs. J. M. Richardson and Miss Laura Baker of Georgetown and Mrs. John Bradley of Elliott; 15 grandchildren and 13 great-grandchildren.

Mr. Baker was one of the oldest members of Trinity Methodist church and had a wide circle of friends here.

Funeral services will be held at the Shelley Brunson Funeral home at 11 o'clock Tuesday morning, followed by interment in the Sumter cemetery.

Obituary from The Sumter Item, Sumter, South Carolina, Monday, October 6, 1940, page 6, column 2. Original newspaper clipping in author's collection.

22

The obituary of my great-great-grandfather, Arthur W. Baker, is packed with family information. It names his parents, siblings, wife, children, and how many grandchildren and great-grandchildren he had. It records spousal information and where everyone was living on a specific day. There are many clues or people to add to the Baker tree. Using the data from the obituary. I could then research down the line to living descendants.

Obituaries are my first go-to record. Due to the nature of the information, there is a good chance clues to descendants will be included. Newspapers are good resources for locating them, but in today's online world, many modern obituaries are placed online and not in traditional papers. Many families opt to place an obituary on a funeral home website. When someone has passed away in the last ten years or so, I usually begin looking by searching the Internet for their name + location + year of death. I have searched for the name + obituary and have had success.

Online resources like FindAGrave.com or other virtual cemeteries can also help. Volunteers and family members create virtual cemeteries by walking through and taking photos of the headstone (if one is still standing) and transcribing records from cemetery records. Once the images and data are collected for the cemetery, a memorial page is made for each individual. Memorial pages include details about the burial place, date of birth and death, and contact details of the person who created and maintains the memorial. Other family members' memorials can be linked together, helping to understand a family unit. Obituaries and more information on the family are often transcribed on the page. Always check if a deceased person on your tree has a memorial and if a family member added an obituary. I have quickly found many in this way—especially those published in newspapers that are unavailable online.

At the bottom of a memorial page is the name of the person who created it, and if transferred to someone else--usually a family member's--their name will appear as the one who maintains the page. Click and go to that person's contact information. They may be who you are looking for!

As with any record, the information on virtual cemeteries is only as reliable as the person who supplied the information. It helps to have a photo of the headstone, but if one is not available, use everything you gather from the memorial page as a clue and look for additional sources to confirm.

Social Columns

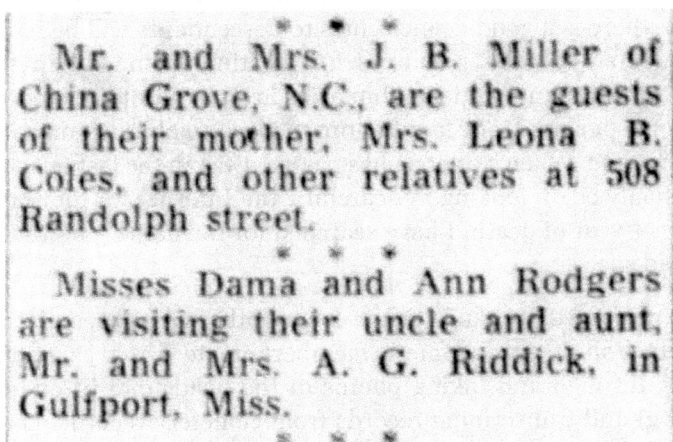

> * ● *
> Mr. and Mrs. J. B. Miller of China Grove, N.C., are the guests of their mother, Mrs. Leona B. Coles, and other relatives at 508 Randolph street.
>
> * * *
>
> Misses Dama and Ann Rodgers are visiting their uncle and aunt, Mr. and Mrs. A. G. Riddick, in Gulfport, Miss.
>
> * * *

Social column announcement from The Huntsville Times. Huntsville, Alabama, Wed., July 20, 1949, page 5, accessed by the author Newspapers.com January 21, 2025

We think we have no privacy today, but there was a time when all the happenings in a community were reported on. From who traveled where and with whom, people coming to town to stay with family members, parties, and other events were recorded, giving clues to connections. Births, deaths, sickness reports, and hospitalizations were written about. There were rumors, gossip, and downright tall tales about community members.

When needing to find the whereabouts of a deceased soldier's granddaughter, I discovered a social column announcing her visit to her grandmother. It was big news that she had traveled from California to the East. The clue of a residence in California led me to find her contact information.

Mrs. Ralph Driggers of Fayetteville, sister of the bride, attended as matron of honor. Attendants were the Misses Nancy Harriu, Laurinburg, N. C.; Johncia Tyndal, Neeces; Brenda Hughes, Florence, sister of the groom.

Wedding announcement from the Florence Morning News, Florence, South Carolina, Sun., August 3, 1975, page 22, accessed by the author on January 1. 2025

News reports of engagements and weddings can be a great source of family information.

Of course, you will find information about the bride, groom, and their parents, but some are very detailed and report on the wedding party and their connections to the family. You will often find the matron and maids of honor, best men and groom, flower girls, and more as part of the bride's or groom's specific family with that connection and where the person is from. Attendees, their relationships, and where they are from can give clues to help you find living descendants.

Schools, Clubs, and Other Events

You never know when your family will be mentioned in the papers. They may attend school, community, and club events. They may be referred to as the child or grandchild of someone in the community. Other guests in attendance for a performance or an award may also be reported on. They may be listed with a group of siblings or cousins who were also participating. Look for any clues that may help you.

Locating Newspapers

An increasing number of newspapers are being digitized and placed online, and many national, state, and local projects are underway. Sites to look for online newspapers in the areas you are researching are Chronicling America, Newspapers.com, Oldnews.com, Newsbank.com, and others. A list of online newspapers is in the appendix of this book. Don't forget to check for digitization projects in specific locations.

Chronicling America, as mentioned previously, has a list of all newspapers published in the United States and the locations where they are held. If you can't find the newspaper you need, look for it and the repository where copies are kept. Then, reach out to the repository to find out how to view the necessary issues. They may be held on microfilm, or there may be original copies. Ask how you can see them. You may need to go in person, or help may be available depending on the facility.

You never know where you may find newspaper articles to help create your tree and research in reverse. Make sure you have talked to and let family members know about the project you are working on and see if they have anything in their possession that may help. Family repositories often contain things that no one knew were there. When my great-aunt died, family members gathered to clean out her home. My dad found several family Bibles in a box in the trash can. Unimaginable to a family historian! He rescued the Bibles and other vital documents, records, and photos. One was her personal Bible. When I received it and opened it, a shower of obituaries, announcements, and other newspaper clippings fell to the floor. Many of those are from papers that are still not digitized.

Many newspapers no longer publish, or only have digital editions with a subscription fee. Some offer a database subscription, allowing access but only for a few articles. Look for engagement, marriage, death notices, and obituaries on social media posts. We will talk about using social media in Chapter 5.

Chapter 3:
Researching Online

The Internet offers many resources and tools for uncovering information about living descendants.

Family Trees

Online family trees such as Ancestry, FamilySearch, MyHeritage, and Findmypast show living people as private on their sites, but there are still ways to identify them.

Look for uploaded public photos that describe who is in the picture. Living individuals are often labeled. When I was looking for a soldier's descendants, a record hint revealed a photo of the soldier's family, with the names of each person in the image. Further research showed the people were his cousins and where they lived. I contacted one of those cousins and asked him to help identify the remains with the help of a Y-DNA test (more about DNA and living relatives to follow in Chapter 7).

The same goes for shared stories, letters, and other documents. The online tree sites automatically mark the living as private when you enter them on the tree. Still, some researchers routinely upload items with living family information, even when their tree is public. Make sure to check any hints uploaded by a family member.

When researching down the line and coming to a deceased person, look for obituaries and other records that indicate this person had descendants. When you come upon a tree that shows there were descendants and is marked as "living," there are still clues to be gathered.

How many private people are there, and what is their relationship to the deceased person? If you are on a site that gives living people a color--blue for male and pink for female--this is an additional clue to the sex of descendants to look for. Don't stop there.

Spouse and children

Sarah Adele Holliday
1914–1990

George "Bubba" Baker
1932–2022

Living Baker

Living Baker

Living Baker

Living Clues 1, Screenshot from Ancestry Tree

The deceased person in this example has living sons. Look for information that will lead to their identities, such as obituaries for the parents, marriage announcements, and other records. Search people finder sites to see if the parents are listed and who may be linked as family members (an in-depth look at people finder sites to follow in Chapter 5).

Remember to click on the living people's icons. You may find a deceased person attached to them. It could be a spouse or a child. The deceased person's records can lead you to names and information to identify the living in a tree. When discovering this scenario, an obituary is a good next step.

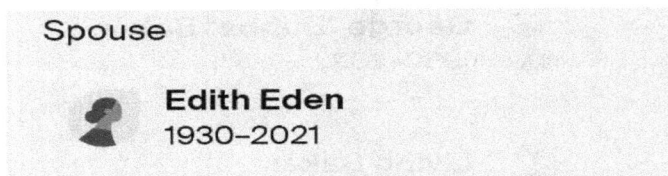

Spouse

Edith Eden
1930–2021

Living Clues 2, screenshot from Ancestry Tree

In this example, clicking on a living person's icon in the tree led to a deceased wife. Her obituary gave the names of her husband and their children. All living people may be able to provide information for genealogy projects.

Public Record Databases

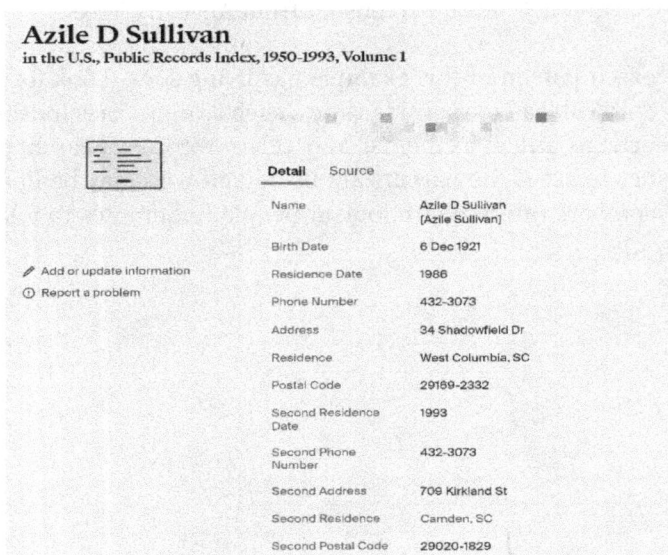

Azile D Sullivan
in the U.S., Public Records Index, 1950-1993, Volume 1

Detail   Source

Name	Azile D Sullivan [Azile Sullivan]
Birth Date	6 Dec 1921
Residence Date	1986
Phone Number	432-3073
Address	34 Shadowfield Dr
Residence	West Columbia, SC
Postal Code	29169-2332
Second Residence Date	1993
Second Phone Number	432-3073
Second Address	709 Kirkland St
Second Residence	Camden, SC
Second Postal Code	29020-1829

✎ Add or update information
ⓘ Report a problem

Sample database page, screenshot from Ancestry.com

Record database sites like Ancestry.com, FamilySearch.org, MyHeritage.com, and FindMyPast.com have public record collections in their catalogs; you may find these records already attached to the family tree you are researching. These collections include directories, property records, yearbooks, and voter registrations.

The hints for public record collections may be on a person's profile page. Search the catalog on the site you use directly through the search box, especially for a particular database, for better results. The search box for a specific collection is created especially for the collection and may return hits that don't show after a search from the main search.

Look through the hints and the catalog, and then search all the available collections. Gather the data on where and when a person lived in a specific area. Learning where people were at one time will help them find where they live now.

Not all the data will be correct. In the example, my grandmother is listed as having lived in Columbia, SC. In this case, her residence was conflated with her older sister, who once lived there. The other homes listed are correct and correlate with other information.

Family Websites

Another place to look for details about living people is on family or surname websites. People place family trees on platforms they have created, which can be found by searching the internet and are open for public viewing. Living people are often not marked as private, and the details of their lives are available. An internet search for the surname of interest may lead you to these sites.

Video or Online Photo Platforms

Use family surnames or keywords like "surname family reunion" in the search bar on platforms like YouTube and Flickr, which can contain family stories or photos uploaded by relatives that contain information on the living.

Public Record Sites

Sample public record site screenshot from the Profession and License Search Page-New Jersey Costumer Affairs website.

Many records are public, open, and free to search. In the United States, there are various ways to locate people. If you are looking for living people in other countries, check to see what types of records are considered public, if any, and how to access them.

States differ in the resources and the availability of the public to view. Still, you can try to locate addresses, phone numbers, and other information to help you contact living family in the following ways.

1. The state board of health may help you find marriage and divorce records. Search for the state and/or county with the keywords "marriage" or "divorce". These records can give you information about the couple and where they lived during the event.

Example:
Iredell County, North Carolina +Divorce returns the link for NC Vital Records: Divorce Certificates. Available from 1958 to present.

2. County Clerk offices may have information on property, deeds, and liens against the property. Search for the county plus property tax or tax assessment. Search for your family to find addresses.

Example: Provo, Utah + Property Records brings up a link for Utah County Government-Web Access to Utah County Land Records. This site includes land records, property, and map search

3. If your research shows someone has or had a public job, use the name of the state or county with public employees or public occupation to find firefighters, policemen, teachers, and anyone working in the public eye.

Example:

Montgomery, Maryland +public employees directs to the Montgomery County Employee Phone Directory.

4. Any occupation requiring a license, such as doctors, attorneys, electricians, etc., might be found by searching for the state and the occupation's name plus license.

Example: Horry County, South Carolina + Beauticians + License shows the link to the South Carolina Cosmetology website. There is a link to look up names of those who have the license with the name and address of where they work.

5. If someone holds or held an elected position, such as mayor, school board, or city council, try searching for the name of the state, county, or city and the elected officials.

Example: Fulton County, Georgia + Elected Officials takes you to the Fulton County Government page with a link to a list of government Officials.

Internet Search Engines

Enter the name of the person of interest and a location in multiple search engines. Algorithms differ, and you may get different results from each. Many modern obituaries can be found online on a funeral home webpage. When looking for a modern obituary, I enter the name, location, year, and obituary in the search bar. Try searching for the person's name plus the location to see if addresses or phone numbers appear in the results. Search for the surname plus genealogy to look for family websites.

Reverse Photo Search

You may come across a photo of a living relative but haven't been able to locate them. Google has a tool called Reverse Photo Search that may help with identification. It will scan an image and look for one that is similar to yours on the Internet. It's a great way to locate people who use the photo on their social media sites and helps you gather contact information.

Here's how to use the feature. On a computer, go to images.google.com. Click on the camera button on the right side of the search bar. It will bring up a popup with options to drag and drop or upload a photo. You can also enter a weblink. Then, click the search button; Google will search for similar images to yours throughout the web. This process can help you find and identify photos of people you wish to contact to help you with your research.

It's especially helpful when you find a profile image and need to identify the person and more information about them. I have used profile pictures from social media, uploaded them for a reverse search and found the same photo on various sites. The information gathered led me to names, addresses, and ways to contact them.

You can also use this method from a cell phone:

1. Go to image.google.com

2. Click on the camera button

3. Click on the images button on the left and choose a photo from your camera roll.

4. Search results will be displayed showing similar photos.

Another option is to take a photo with your phone and use that to perform a reverse search.

Chapter 4:
Researching On Location

Not all genealogical information is online. Libraries, archives, and historical societies hold many records that might help you find living family members. Local libraries often have old newspapers, city directories, and yearbooks that provide clues about where people lived and who they associated with.

Places to Contact or Visit

Historical societies may have family files, local histories, or even unpublished manuscripts that include information about your relatives. Don't hesitate to ask the staff for guidance when visiting these places. They can often point you to resources you might not have considered.

Libraries are often the hub of a community, especially in small towns. They may have a dedicated room for genealogy and local histories with resources to help with research. Always ask to speak to those who have worked there for an extended period and are experts in the area. They may be able to connect you with family who are still living there.

Genealogical societies can be good sources of information. Some have a research room that contains records donated to them. Some members are researchers, have experience with the sources available, and are experts in the location. They may be able to point you to resources and living family members.

Museums are more than just a place to visit to see artifacts about a community or event, a museum also has extensive knowledge about a community, time frame, or event. Some have record collections open to the public.

What to Look For

Phone books: Many communities are still publishing phone books or directories.

Recently published information will be more correct than older editions and online information.

Yearbooks: Look for more recent dates, and for people with the surnames you are researching. Collect the names and see what you can learn about them and if they are connected to your line.

Publications: Ask if they hold original or microfilmed local newspapers, magazines, newsletters from local churches and organizations, and other books that may help you.

Hanging files: As the name suggests, these files are placed in filing cabinets. They contain information on surnames, locations, businesses, schools, churches, and any other topic about a community. Hanging files are labeled, and as people find information about the various subjects, the clippings, genealogy charts, copies of photos, and any other item that would help others learn about the topic or connect with other people researching the surnames and the area. When you visit, bring your pedigree chart to place in a surname file and copies of photos and documents to share with others who look through the file. Don't forget your name, address, and phone number so others can contact you.

Family Collections

Family photo from author's personal collection

Don't forget to see what you or other family members already have. Look at family photos for clues to descendants you have not researched. Look in photo albums, scrapbooks, and framed pictures on the furniture or hanging on the walls. Analyze them. How many people are in the family? Does it look like a family unit? How many children or grandchildren are pictured? It would be nice if the photos were labeled, but there are ways to identify unknown people. Show them to older family members, upload them to Facebook genealogy groups, and ask if anyone can determine who is in the photo, create a blog post to get the image out for people to see. The same holds for family movies! Gather the older generations, pop some corn, and sit back and enjoy as you gather clues.

Look for diaries, journals, and letters. These may have names, dates, places, and stories about the family members you already have in your tree and for the descendants you are looking for.

My grandmother kept an address book. It included many friends and family with their addresses at the time. Building on old addresses and correlating them with newer ones found in an online search, I verified the correct contact information for a third cousin.

Remember to ask your family! We often fail to ask about collateral lines and descendants of our ancestors' siblings, aunts, uncles, and cousins as we work to research down our tree.

Chapter 5:
People Finders and Social Media

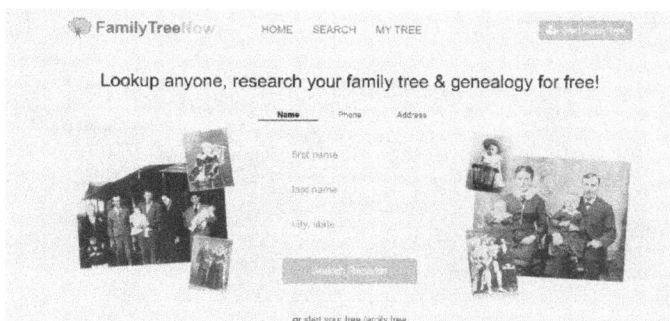

Screenshot of Search Page from FamilyTreeNow

Databases are great. They can give you a history of where people may have been, but the best way to discover where they are now is by using an online people finder like BeenVerified.com, FamilyTreeNow.com, TruePeopleSearch.com, Spokeo.com, and White Pages.com.

Some are free, and others are subscription-based. Many have free trials. They work by aggregating and compiling information on a person in one place, giving addresses, phone numbers, email, and social media information. Think about it as an online private eye helping you. They are simple to use.

Enter what you know about an individual in the search box. Typically, it would help if you had a name, approximate age, and last known location. Much of this you have learned previously. After a search, look at the results and choose the one that best fits the information previously discovered on the person. Run a search on several sites as they work differently, and their search engines may bring back different information. Piecing those bits of information together can help puzzle out someone's whereabouts. If you doubt whether this is your person, compare the addresses and family members to what you have learned. You should see familiar family members and the same pattern of residences.

A technique that can help connect families on these sites is to search for a deceased person. Click on family members to see who is associated with them. Many platforms have recently linked obituaries to a deceased person's profile.

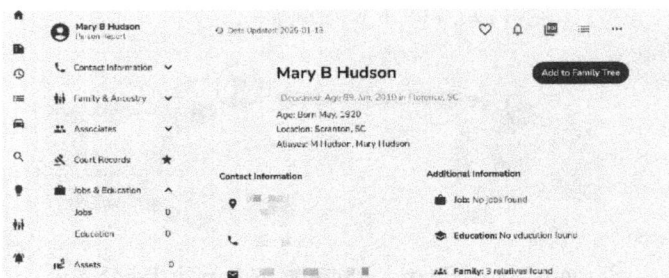

Screenshot from BeenVerified.com
Deceased PersonResults.

Addresses have a "date seen" next to them. The later dates are not guaranteed to be correct, but they are a better choice than ones from decades ago. Click on the address and look at the property information. Is your person the owner? When did they buy the property? Who else is listed as a resident or owner? Correlate this with other location facts to build confidence in the current address. Send a letter explaining who you are and your purpose for contacting them. It helps to include a family chart to show how you are related.

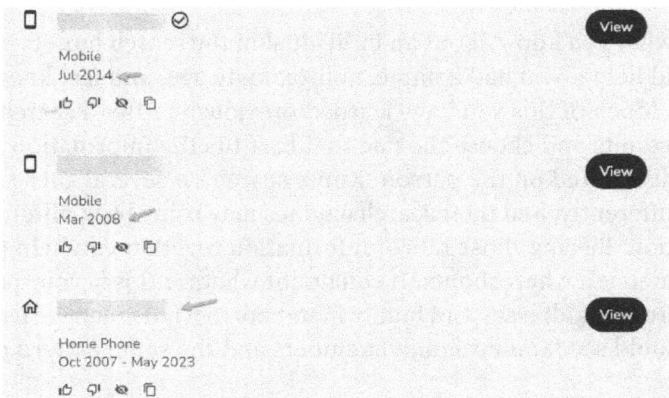

Screenshot from BeenVerified.com of Dates Seen

Phone numbers will have the same "date seen" type of information as addresses. They will also indicate whether it is a cell number or a landline. In my experience, many of these numbers are not correct. The only way to know is to call. If you find a correct number and someone answers, be very thankful! Today, people are suspicious of unknown numbers calling them and will not take the call.

Leave a voicemail, whether there is a recording identifying the owner of the number or not, explaining why you are calling and letting them know you are looking for family to help with genealogy research. Make it clear that you are not making a sales call and that your call is not spam. Some phone numbers are set up not to take calls, and although they are working numbers, you will get a notification saying either they do not have a voicemail or the number is not working. Try texting the number to see if a message will go through.

Another way to find an address or phone number is to look for those listed as family members. Not everyone on the list is an actual family member, and not all family members are included, but there should be one or two you recognize from your earlier research. Spouses and parents, living or deceased, usually make the list.

Click on their names, especially spouses. What are the addresses and phone numbers associated with those names? If the phone numbers of the individual you are searching for are incorrect, see if a spouse has a number you haven't tried. Typically, spouses have different cell phone numbers, and you may be able to get in touch that way. Since children would be part of the family you are researching, see if their numbers are correct. You can try to contact them by mail too. Hopefully, they will want to help you and contact their parents.

The names of associates are also listed. These are typically people mentioned in records or maybe neighbors, friends, or work colleagues. If you have difficulty locating correct addresses or phone numbers, contact people from that list to see if they can help you.

Social Media

Social media platforms like Facebook, Instagram, and others can also be powerful tools for finding people. Many people do not keep their social media information private; anyone can view their About page, friends list, and feed. Look for clues to where someone lives and who their family members are. Correlate this information with what you learned in other searches. Look for family photos with captions and comments describing relationships. Send a message through the platform system along with details about who you are and why you would like to communicate with them. If the person does not respond, reach out to family members in their friends list and those identified as family in descriptions and comments. Search screenshot, Google Search Results for the author.

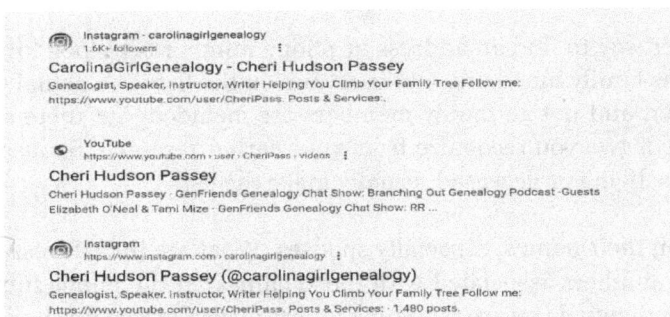

Screenshot of Username Search Results for the Author

I located a person I needed to contact for a case by searching his wife's social media username, which was included in a BeenVerified report. The search resulted in a hit for someone with that username on Instagram. One of her posts was a picture of her with her husband, whom she identified. I sent her a private message explaining my purpose in contacting her.

Then, I looked for her on Facebook, found her there, and sent her the same message. She responded and connected me with her husband, who helped me with the case I was working on. Don't forget to look for genealogy Facebook groups in the areas where your family is from. Post a query asking if anyone knows the family and will help you connect with them.

Chapter 6:
Reaching Out to Family

In today's world, people tend to be suspicious of unsolicited contact. Mail, including email, is often unopened or unread, phone calls are not responded to, and queries from unknown people trying to contact through social media can be fearful for some. We are all trying to protect ourselves from spam, scams, stalkers, and other nefarious situations. There are ways to increase your chances of connecting with those willing to help you with your research.

No matter which way you reach out, begin by introducing yourself and your purpose for making contact.

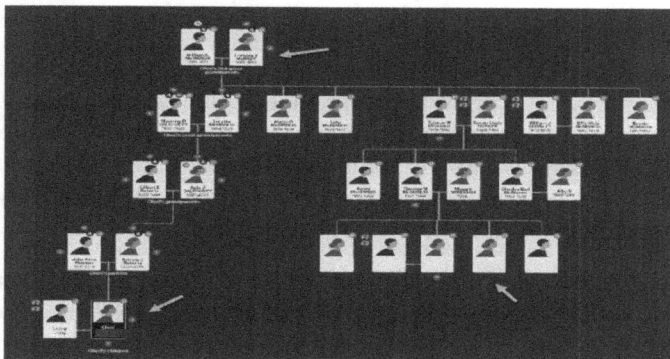

Common Ancestor Chart, screenshot from Ancestry showing common ancestors.

When sending a letter or email, include a business card, the link to a family website, blog, or anything else to introduce yourself as a legitimate family researcher. A copy of a chart showing where the two of you fit in the family tree can be beneficial. If you can find someone already on a family tree site, it may be easier to get in touch using the platform's message service. Many people report frustration when sending these messages, and the person doesn't answer. Still, I have had better success when I reach out, giving them information on who I am, how I fit in within the family, and my purpose for contacting them. I also share my email address in the message so they know I am serious and encourage further communication.

Cold calling can be tricky. If no one answers, leave a detailed message. Give your name and why you are calling, and explain that you are a family researcher who is looking to connect with them. Tell them how you are related. After introducing myself, one of the first things I say is that my call is about family history and not a solicitation so that the person can be more at ease. If the person is still unsure, offer to send them an email or letter with the information about your connection.

People like to know how helping you will help them, especially those not involved in family history. Let them know that, through their efforts to tell what they know or have documents, photos, family bibles, stories, etc., helping you discover more about your shared family lines will help you uncover more ancestors and family stories. Tell them you will keep them updated on how what they share is helping your research and any discoveries you are led to due to their help. Make it clear that you are not asking for original items to be given to you, but would appreciate copies.

It is also essential to inform those you contact that you understand and honor the ethics of information about living people. Describe the policies of family tree sites regarding keeping living people added to a tree private. If they have something they do not want to be shared publicly, such as a photo, document, story, or DNA results, comply with that request.

Be prepared for a negative response or no response at all. Be patient and courteous. No one owes us anything, and they have the choice to help or not. A kind word from you may lead to wanting to help later once they have had time to think it through or decide to pursue building a tree of their own.

Don't leave a bad impression. You never know when someone may change their mind and reach out.

Chapter 7:
A Word About DNA

DNA testing is a powerful tool for finding living relatives. There are three main types of DNA tests:

1. **Autosomal DNA tests** connect relatives from both your mother's and father's sides.

2. **Y-DNA tests** trace direct paternal lines for men, helping to trace a line back or determine who someone's biological father. and to connect with other males from a paternal line. YDNA is also used to identify the remains of a deceased male.

3. **Mitochondrial DNA (mtDNA) tests** trace direct maternal lines and can be taken by everyone. Although women pass on maternal DNA, a mother also passes her mtDNA to her daughters and sons. It ends there. A son can not pass on maternal DNA, but daughters will continue to pass it on. These tests are used to trace maternal lines, connect with other females in a family line, and identify the remains of both men and women.

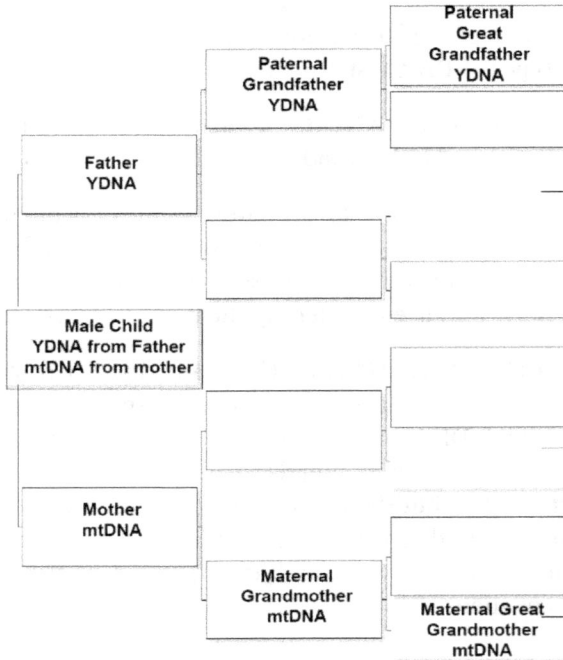

		Paternal Great Grandfather YDNA
	Paternal Grandfather YDNA	
Father YDNA		
Male Child YDNA from Father mtDNA from mother		
Mother mtDNA		
	Maternal Grandmother mtDNA	
		Maternal Great Grandmother mtDNA

A male cannot pass on the mtDNA he
gets from his maternal line.

Male mtDNA and YDNA inheritance Pathway.

Chart created by Author.

Female mtDNA Pathway

A Mother passes mtDNA to her sons and daughters

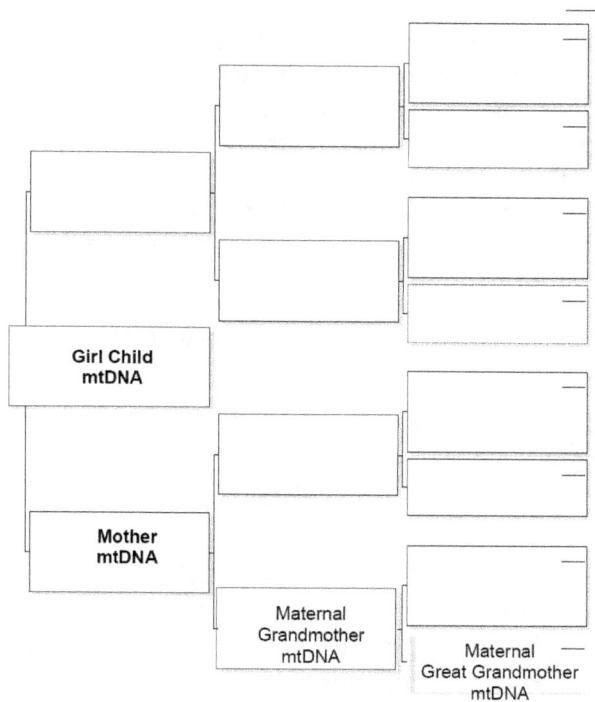

Girl Child mtDNA

Mother mtDNA

Maternal Grandmother mtDNA

Maternal Great Grandmother mtDNA

Female mtDNA Inheritance Pathway.

Chart Created by Author.

Create a plan for whom you are looking and what type of DNA test could provide connections to the living. A list of DNA companies is included in the Tools and Resources pages at the end of this book.

When asking someone to take a DNA test, explain how it works and why it's essential for the project you are working on. Create a chart showing your objective and how their DNA can help. Be sensitive to privacy concerns and offer to cover the test cost if necessary. Let them know how their participation can help expand the family story and that you will keep them informed on how the project is going. Offer to explain their results, what they mean, and how they are helping you come to conclusions about your shared family.

DNA testing comes with risks. Results may be unexpected and, for some, life-changing.

Explain this clearly to anyone willing to test for you. They may find out something they did not want to know. Test takers need to be aware of and prepared for what may be the result of taking any type of DNA test.

When searching for the living, whether a DNA test is needed depends on your purpose. Positive identification for repatriation, biological parents, and determining connections to ancestors require a DNA test. If you are looking for living cousins to help you with documents, photos, stories and heirlooms, you may not need it.

Chapter 8:
Working Through a Soldier Repatriation Case: Steps for Finding Living Family

Although the names of the Soldiers and their families are private, these are the steps and actions I take to locate living family for a Soldier. The goal is to discover the primary and secondary next of kin to make decisions about burial if identification is made, and three mtDNA and one YDNA living family members to make that identification. mtDNA is the primary way remains are identified, therefore the need for more than one sample. Note: DNA protocols are subject to change as testing procedures are updated.

A repatriation case begins when documents are provided giving me the name of a Soldier, his birth and death dates, those who were recorded as next of kin when he enlisted, and other clues about locations and pertinent information to help me begin a family tree. Most of these are parents or siblings. I work on WWII cases, so the original next of kin have passed away, as well as brothers and sisters. There has been a time or two when a Soldier had a very large family with the youngest sibling still alive. I begin the tree with the Soldier and any family members mentioned in his military records and begin looking for their records. First, I look to see if the Soldier was married and had children and grandchildren. Locating and contacting these direct descendants is always a positive experience. They know the story of their father or grandfather and want to help with the case.
My most memorable find was a daughter who, when I contacted her, was in the middle of planning her 85 birthday! She said my call was the best birthday present she could think of.

Next, I research any siblings and their children. Nieces and nephews are often the next of kin. Their birth year determines whether they are the **primary**, the oldest, and the **secondary**, the next oldest. I go through this process through the Soldier's descendants to locate a living person who qualifies for the next of kin role.

If I am lucky, the next of kin also qualifies as a DNA donor. Many times, they do not. Descendants of a brother may only be female and descendants of a sister may have males that could not pass mtDNA to their children.

When that's the case, and no one down the line has the correct DNA for testing, I head up. That means I look for the Soldier's grandparents, aunts, and uncles. Paternal lines may have daughters out, and maternal lines may only have had sons, taking me up the generations and back down again to try to locate a living person with the correct DNA. Using census records, obituaries, and any other record available, I add people to the Soldier's tree, hoping one of the collateral lines can be traced to a living person. These often end up being distantly related to the Soldier, but the DNA is just as good at doing the job as close ties.

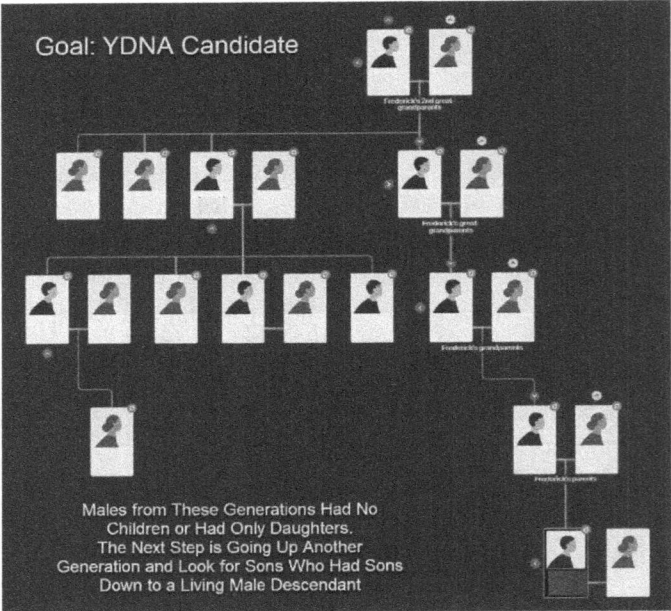

Researching up and then coming back down the tree, screenshot from Ancestry Looking for YDNA.

The next step is to find contact information for the potential DNA donor. I gather information on former or current residences using online databases, look for spouses and children to add to the tree, and other data available to help me locate them.

I then turn to people-finder websites to find current information. I scroll through the search results and look for the best possible match. The pages for an individual show birth dates, names, maiden names for women, previous and current locations, names or maiden names for women, and other family members—clues to help determine if you have found the correct person.

Next, I check the list of addresses and phone numbers to look for the most recent ones. They are not always correct, but I have had good luck reaching the right person when sending a letter or making a call and explaining the need for help with the case.

Do they always respond? No. Sometimes, I have to reach out to the spouses or children of my contact person. There are times when I get no response. In that event, if a priority signature-required letter has been accepted and delivered, or a voicemail identifies a phone number, the information is passed on, and the Army takes it from there.

Looking for your living family members takes the same steps:

1. Build an accurate tree for the line you are researching.

2. Search for records to help you find information leading you to living people.
Remember, often, you have to go up the tree and come back down collateral lines.

3. Once a living descendant is identified, search for contact information.

4. Use best practices for communicating with those who may be willing to help you with your research.

Conclusion

Finding living relatives can be an exciting and rewarding part of genealogy. Combining traditional research methods with modern tools and a respectful approach can uncover new stories, build meaningful connections, and enrich your understanding of your family history.

Genealogy is about more than just names and dates—it's about people and their stories. With the strategies in this book, you have everything you need to find living family by doing genealogy in reverse.

Tools and Resources for Genealogy in Reverse

Cemetery Resources
- **BillionGraves** (https://www.billiongraves.com)

- **FindAGrave** (https://www.findagrave.com)

DNA Testing Services
- **23AndMe** (https://www.23andme.com/)
  Note: At the time this book was going to print,
  23andMe filed for bankruptsey. The future of the company is
  not clear.
- **AncestryDNA** (https://www.ancestry.com/dna)

- **FamilyTreeDNA** (https://www.familytreedna.com)

- **MyHeritageDNA** (https://www.myheritage.com/dna)

Genealogy Computer Software Programs
- **FamilyTreeMaker** (https://www.mackiev.com/ftm)

- **Heredis** (https://www.heredis.com)

- **Legacy Family Tree**
  (https://www.legacyfamilytree.com)

- **RootsMagic** (https://www.rootsmagic.com)

Genealogy Tree and Research Platforms

- **Ancestry** (https://www.ancestry.com)

- **FamilySearch** (https:??www.familysearch.org)

- **Findmypast** (https://www.findmypast.com)

- **MyHeritage** (https://www.myheritage.com)

- **WikiTree** (https://www.wikitree.com)

Online Organization Tools

- **Evernote** (https://www.evernote.com)
- **Goldie May** (https://www.goldiemay.com)
- **Google Docs** https://(docs.google.com)
- **Trello** (https://www.trello.com)

People Finder Websites

- **BeenVerified** (https://www.beenverified.com)
- **FamilyTreeNow** (https://www.familytreenow.com)
- **Spokeo** https://(www.spokeo.com)
- **TruePeopleSearch** (https://www.truepeoplesearch.com)
- **Whitepages** (https://www.whitepages.com)

Social Media

- **Facebook** (https://www.facebook.com)
- **Flicker** (https://www.facebook.com)
- **Instagram (https://www.instagram.com)**
- **YouTube** (https://www.youtube.com

Other:

- **Genealogical Proof Standard** (https://www.bcgcertification.org/ethics-standards#genea-logical-proof-standard-gps)